MAKING CLOTHES

Felicity Everett and Carol Garbera
Illustrated by Sara Silcock and Christine Berrington

Designed by Camilla Luff

Edited by Angela Wilkes

CONTENTS

With thanks to John Garbera & Bill Le Fever

About this book

Making your own clothes is enjoyable and a lot easier than you might think. It gives you a wide range of styles and fabrics to choose from and is cheaper than buying things ready made. This book gives you patterns for a colourful range of co-ordinated clothes you will want to make and wear, and shows you step-by-step how to make them. Some of the patterns are simple and others more difficult, but they are all easy to follow. The book covers all the basic dressmaking skills you need to know, from start to finish, and also tells you how to make your own patterns.

The patterns

The patterns in this book are designed to fit sizes 10 and 12. Each pattern is printed on a chart at the end of the sewing instructions. Follow the black outline for size 10 and the red one for size 12. You can find out how to draw the patterns to scale on pages 6 and 7. There are diagrams for suggested fabric layouts next to the patterns. All the layouts are for fabrics with naps.

Things you need

Your sewing machine

You need a sewing machine to make the clothes. Turn to pages 4 and 5 to find out more about sewing machines and how to thread them.

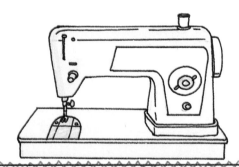

For making the patterns

Here are the things you need to make your own patterns. You can find out what to do on pages 6 and 7.

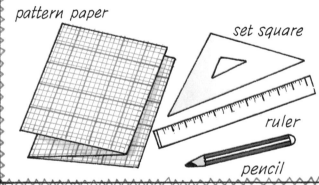

pattern paper

set square

ruler

pencil

For pressing

An iron and ironing board are almost as important as your sewing machine when you are making clothes. You can find out why on page 11.

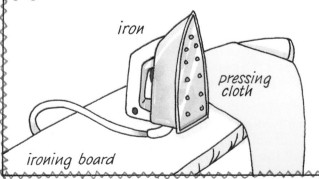

iron

pressing cloth

ironing board

Your sewing box

These are the general things you need for dressmaking. You can buy them in the haberdashery departments of large stores. Keep the dressmaking scissors for cutting fabric and make sure your pins and needles do not get rusty.

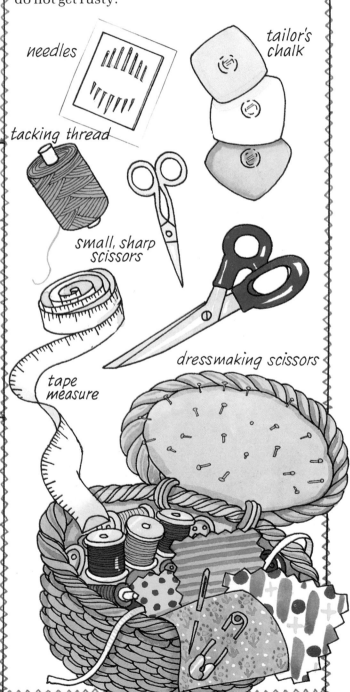

needles

tailor's chalk

tacking thread

small, sharp scissors

tape measure

dressmaking scissors

Your sewing machine

You need a sewing machine to make the clothes in this book. Electric machines are faster, but a hand machine will do. Put your machine on a table in a well-lit room or near a bright lamp.

Your machine may not look exactly the same as the one shown here. Check your machine handbook if you are not sure where things are. Try your machine out on scraps of fabric before you make anything.

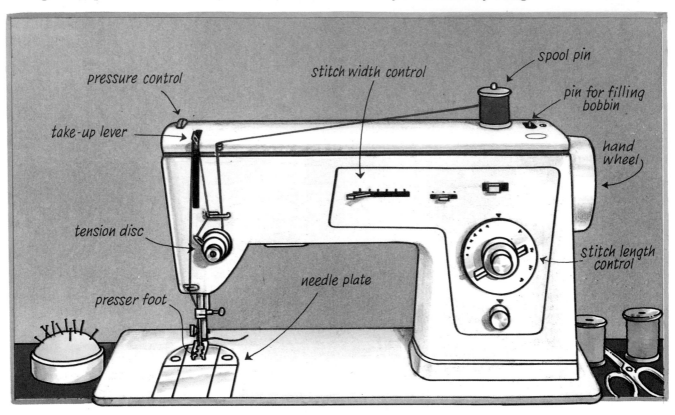

Filling the bobbin

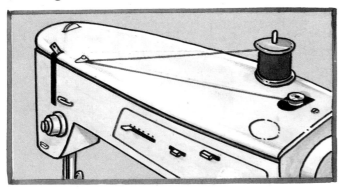

Put a reel of thread and the empty bobbin on the machine as shown. Pass the end of the thread round the clip and wind it a few times round the bobbin. Loosen the handwheel, work the machine until the bobbin is full and then cut the thread. Tighten the handwheel.

Threading the bobbin case

1. Slot the bobbin into the case as shown. Keep the end of the thread free of the case.

2. Pull the thread down the groove and under the clip.

3. Open the bobbin case handle and slot the case into position under the needle plate.

Check your machine handbook to find out what to do if your machine has a built-in bobbin case.

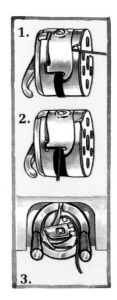

Threading the machine

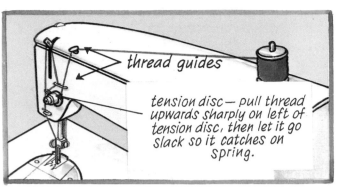

thread guides

tension disc — pull thread upwards sharply on left of tension disc, then let it go slack so it catches on spring.

Raise the presser foot. Put the reel of thread on the spool pin and guide the thread around the loops as shown in the picture. Thread the needle from left to right or from front to back, depending on the type of machine.

Raising the bobbin thread

1. Hold the top thread in your left hand and slowly turn the handwheel with your right until the needle picks up a loop of thread from the bottom bobbin.

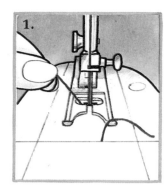

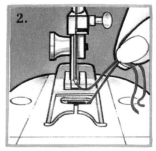

2. Gently pull both threads out and push them under the presser foot. Leave ends about 10cm long.

Tension

The tension is the amount of 'give' in the thread. If the thread is too tight, the seam puckers. If it is too slack, the stitches are loopy. The tension is right when the stitches form in the middle of the fabric.

tension too tight

tension too loose

tension correct

You can adjust the tension by turning the tension disc on the machine. Different fabrics need different tension. Check it on scraps of fabric until it is right.

Needle sizes

Sizes range from 9 (finest) to 18 (thickest). Use special ball-point needles for sewing jersey fabrics. A sharp point may divide the strand of yarn and spoil the fabric. The lighter the fabric, the finer the needle you should use. Use size 11 or 14 for medium-weight fabrics.

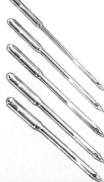

Pressure

Some machines have a pressure control which helps to feed the fabric evenly through the machine. The thinner the fabric, the lighter the pressure needed.

Stitches

You can alter the stitch length or width by adjusting the controls on the machine (see picture on facing page).

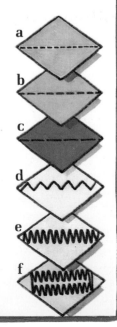

a For running stitch, set stitch width control at 0.

b A medium stitch length is suitable for most fabrics.

c Use the longest stitch length for gathering.

d,e Use zig zag stitches for sewing stretch fabrics. You have to adjust both the stitch length and width for these.

f When you are sewing buttonholes, use the shortest stitch length and a wide stitch width.

Making the patterns

The patterns in this book are printed in chart form on grids. Here you can find out how to scale them up on to pattern paper to make your own patterns. It is much easier than you might think.

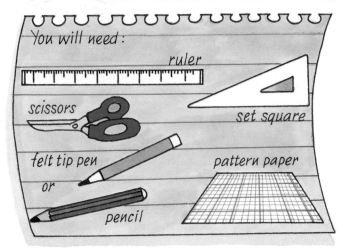

You will need:
ruler
scissors
set square
felt tip pen
or
pencil
pattern paper

Pattern paper

You can buy special paper for making your own patterns in the haberdashery sections of fabric shops and department stores. It looks like grid paper marked into 1cm and 5cm squares. If you cannot buy the paper you can make your own. You will need large sheets of brown paper, a pencil, a ruler and a set square.

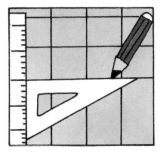

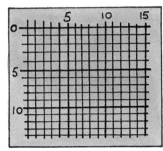

First divide your paper into 5cm squares. Rule lengthwise lines first, then crosswise ones, using a set square to make sure they cross at right angles.

Divide each big square into 25 1cm squares, then mark every fifth square down the side and across the top, as shown, starting in the top left corner.

Things to remember

The scale of the charts to the patterns is 1 to 5. This means that a 1cm square on the chart = a 5cm square on the pattern paper. A 2mm square on the chart = a 1cm square on the pattern paper.

There are outlines for sizes 10 and 12 on each pattern. Size 10 is outlined in black and size 12 in red. Make sure you copy out the right outline for your size.

The symbols on the patterns are called construction marks. You can find out what they mean on the opposite page. You use tailor tacks to mark them on the fabric (see page 9).

Making a pattern

Collect everything you need before you start. If your pattern paper is creased, iron it with a cool iron, then spread it out on a table or on the floor.

Draw the big pattern pieces first. Mark crosses on the paper where the widest and longest points of each piece come. Draw a box through them.

Using the big squares as a rough guide and the small ones to fix the exact position, draw crosses where the pattern piece meets the box.

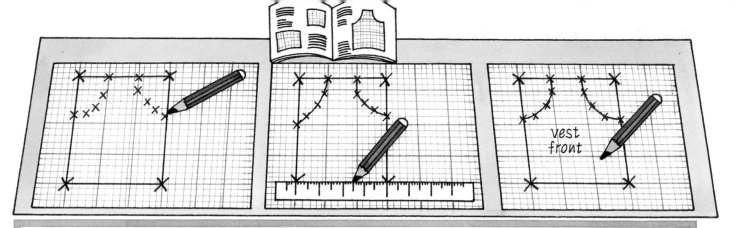

Plot the precise outline of the piece by making a cross at each point where the outline of the pattern piece crosses the grid lines of the paper.

Using a ruler for the straight lines, join the centres of the crosses together to make an even cutting line. Draw the curves carefully and slowly.

Check the number of big squares on your pattern against the number of squares on the chart. Write the name of the pattern piece on it.

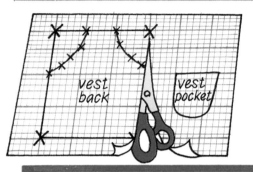

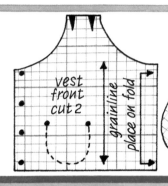

Draw the rest of the pattern pieces in the same way, fitting the smaller pattern pieces between the big pieces. Then cut them all out.

Copy everything that is on the pattern chart on to your pattern pieces, including the number of times you should cut out each piece.

Give each pattern piece a letter (so you know if you lose one) then put them in an envelope and write the name of the pattern on the front.

Construction marks

Notches help you match one piece of a garment to another, e.g. a collar to a shirt.

You use dots to match seamlines when joining two pieces of a garment together and to mark pocket positions.

Darts look like this. You can find out how to stitch them on page 11.

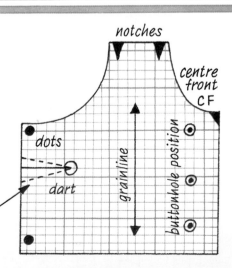

The centre front and centre back of a pattern are often marked to help you position other pattern pieces in line with them.

Always line the grainline up with the straight grain of the fabric – parallel to the selvedges.

Pattern pieces which are to be placed on a fold have arrows to show which edge goes on the fold.

Getting ready

When you are making clothes it is worth taking the time to prepare and cut out the fabric carefully, so that your clothes hang well. If you cut out the fabric in a hurry it is very easy to make expensive mistakes. Below you can find out how to start.

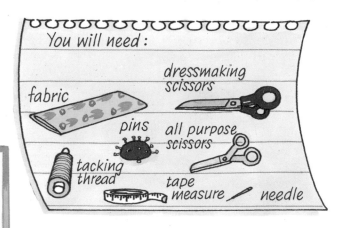

You will need: fabric, dressmaking scissors, pins, all purpose scissors, tacking thread, tape measure, needle

Preparing the pattern pieces

Patterns from shops give you all the pieces on big sheets of paper. You have to cut them out roughly before you can pin them down. Smooth out the pattern paper with a warm iron if it is creased.

Preparing the fabric

If your fabric is creased, press it well. Stretchy fabrics should be left spread out overnight so they can 'relax'.

If you are using cotton, or another fabric which might shrink, it is a good idea to wash and iron it before you lay it out.

If your fabric has not been cut off the roll in a straight line, straighten the edge as follows.

Put a set square flat along the selvedge and hold a ruler along the top, as shown. Draw a chalk line across the fabric and cut along it.

Fabrics with a nap

For a fabric with a nap or a one-way design, you must lay out all the pattern pieces with the nap or pattern facing the same way. If the pattern layout shows a widthways fold, cut along the fold, then lay the two pieces of fabric wrong sides together, making sure that the nap or pattern runs the same way on both pieces.

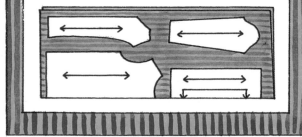

Understanding the pattern layout

All patterns give recommended pattern layouts. In this book they are on the same page as the pattern.

There is usually a different layout for each fabric width. The layout shows you where to fold the fabric and put each pattern piece.

Checks and stripes

Avoid checks and stripes if you are a beginner as they have to match at all seams and this is difficult to do. If you want to use a striped or checked fabric, choose a simple pattern and remember to match seams on the seamline, not the cutting line.

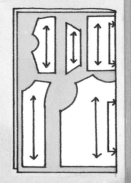

Cutting out

Fold the fabric and arrange the pattern pieces as shown on your layout. Make sure they all fit before you pin them down. For a napped fabric, see opposite page.

If a pattern piece says 'cut 2 to pair', cut it out once, then turn the pattern piece over and cut it out again, so you have a right and a left piece.

Position each piece so the grainline runs along the straight grain of the fabric*. Measure from the selvedge to make sure it is straight.

Pin the grainline in position first, then smooth the pattern outwards and pin round the edges. Put the pins in at right angles to the pattern piece.

Before you start cutting out, make sure that you have not missed out any pattern pieces and check the right ones are on the double layer of fabric.

Cut each piece out carefully. When you come to a notch, cut it outwards instead of into the seam allowance. Cut double and triple notches in a block.

Leave the pattern pinned to the fabric until you have transferred the dots on to the fabric using tailor tacks. You can see how to do this below.

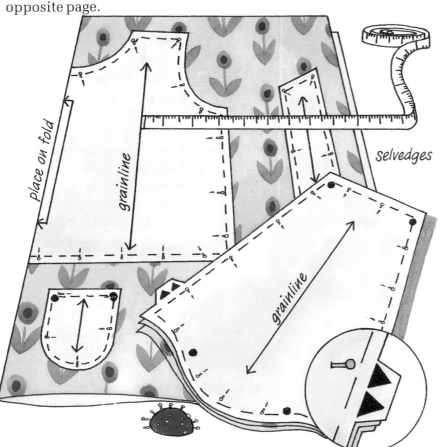

place on fold

grainline

selvedges

grainline

notches

Making tailor tacks

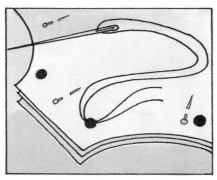

With a double length of unknotted thread, stitch through the pattern and both layers of fabric. Leave ends about 2.5cm long.

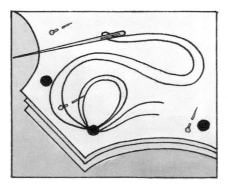

Backstitch in the same place to make a loop. Cut the thread about 2.5cm from the fabric, as shown. Cut the loop and lift the pattern away from the fabric.

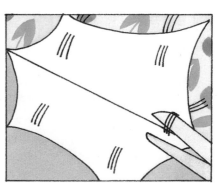

Gently separate the two layers of fabric and cut the threads in between to leave a few tufts of thread in each piece. These are your tailor tacks.

* See page 45

Making seams and darts

As clothes are held together by seams, you must make them strong and neaten the raw edges so they do not fray. There are different kinds of seam, but the type shown below is the one you will need to use most often.

Darts are used to give shape and fullness to clothes. The clothes in this book do not have darts, but it is useful to know how to make them.

The seam allowance

The seam allowance is the distance between the edge of the fabric and the seamline (the line you stitch along). Your pattern tells you what the seam allowance is. You will find it easier to sew straight along the seamline if you line up the edge of your fabric with one of the grooves in the needle plate of your machine.

Pinning

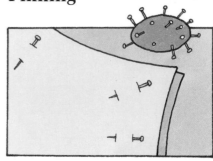

Always use clean, sharp pins. Blunt, rusty ones make holes in the fabric. Pin the edges of the fabric together, putting the pins in at right angles to the edge.

Tacking

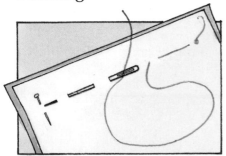

Starting with a knot or a couple of stitches, tack close to the seamline. Take the pins out as you tack, and finish off with a single backstitch.

Machining

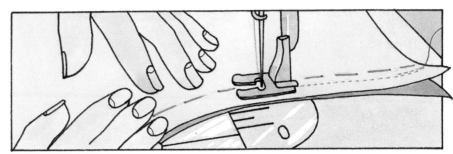

Check that your sewing machine has the right size needle in it and is set to the right tension and pressure. Try the stitching on a scrap of fabric.

Check the seam allowance and put the needle in on the seamline. Backstitch at the beginning and stitch along the seamline. Backstitch at the end.

Neatening Seams

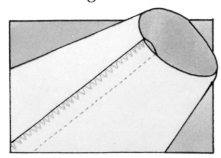

If the seam allowance is narrow, machine the raw edges together with a short, wide zigzag. Press the seam towards the back or body of the garment.

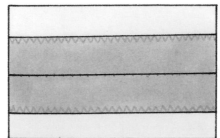

For a wider seam allowance, zigzag stitch each edge separately or oversew them by hand (see p. 42), then press them apart.

For firmly woven fabric which does not fray easily you can neaten the raw edges by trimming them with pinking shears to give a zigzag edge.

Darts

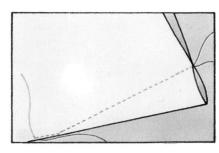

Mark the position of the dart with tailor tacks (see page 9). Fold and pin it as shown, then tack it from the wide edge to the point and take out the pins.

Stitch from wide edge to the point. Make the last few stitches right on the edge of the fold, so that the dart lies flat on the right side of the fabric.

Tie the ends of the thread in a knot to secure your stitching (backstitching makes the point of the dart too bulky). Press the dart to one side.

Pressing

When you are sewing, you should press each piece of stitching you do, especially seams and darts, to make sure they lie flat. Put the ironing board up before you start sewing, so you can press things as you go along.

Before you press your sewing, take out the pins and tacking. Test the heat of the iron on a spare piece of the fabric.

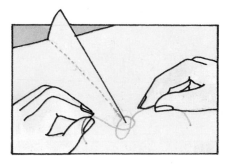

Temperature guide

 hot iron (cotton, linen, viscose)

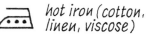 warm iron (polyester, mixtures, wool)

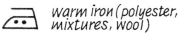 cool iron (synthetics)

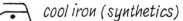 do not iron

A steam iron is best for pressing. If you do not have one, use a damp cloth, especially for thick fabrics such as wool and tweed and fabrics which crease badly, such as linen. It is best to press things on the wrong side.

Use the tip of the iron to open up seams and get into the corners. Press curved seams on the end of your ironing board with the tip of your iron.

Pressing is not the same as ironing. Gently lower the iron on to the area to be pressed and then lift it off again. Do not slide it across the fabric.

11

Cotton vest

This vest is the easiest thing in the book to make. It is a clingy style which looks best made in jersey fabric.

Sizes

To fit chest: 83/87cm
Finished size
chest: 85/90cm
length: 56/59cm

Sewing jersey

Try not to stretch the fabric as you are stitching it.

Use a medium ballpoint needle*

Stitch seams with a short, narrow zigzag stitch.

Make the pattern, following the chart on page 15, and cut it out. Then cut out the fabric.

Suggested fabrics

Cotton jersey, stretch towelling, silky jersey.

Pocket

Neaten the top edge of the pocket with a short, wide zigzag stitch. Turn in 1.5cm along the top. Tack and press. Stitch close to neatened edge**

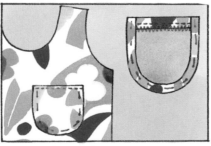

Turn in 5mm round rest of pocket. Tack and press. Pin the pocket on vest front so its top edge lines up with tailor tacks on front. Tack. Topstitch.

Topstitching

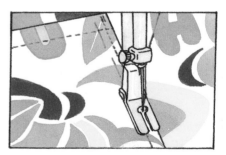

Position the presser foot of machine so the stitching comes 1-2mm from the edge of the pocket. Stitch round pocket, leaving top edge free.

* See page 5   ** Set stitch width control at 0 for running stitch.

Shoulder and side seams

Pin front and back of vest together at shoulder and side seams, with right sides together. Tack in place, taking pins out as you go.

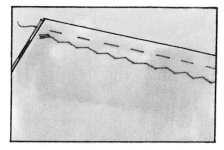

Set the zigzag on your sewing machine to a medium length, narrow width setting. Stitch the seams. Backstitch at start and finish.

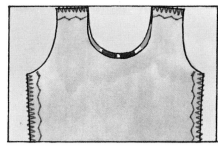

Change the stitch setting back to the short, wide zigzag you used for the top edge of the pocket and stitch the seam edges together to neaten them.

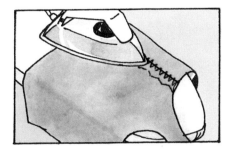

Take out the tacking stitches. Using a warm iron, press the neatened edges of the seams towards the back of the vest along the seamline.

Finishing the neck and sleeves

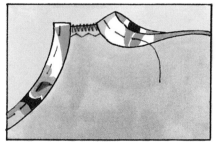

Turn in 5mm round the neck and armholes. Tack and press. Turn in another 1cm to cover the raw edges. Tack and press in place.

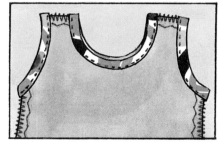

With your machine set at a medium stitch length, straight stitch round the neck and sleeve openings about 2mm from the inner folded edge.

Hemming

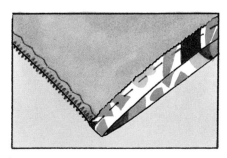

Turn in 5mm round the bottom edge of the vest, as you did to finish the armholes and neck. Tack and press turning in place, as shown.

Measure 1.5cm in from the first turning and make a second one. Tack and press. Stitch it in place about 2mm in from the inner folded edge.

Appliqué vest

Here you can find out how to sew a letter or number on your vest.

You will need

60-70cm of fabric as for vest
piece of contrast colour fabric (cotton, satin or poplin) 25cm × 25cm
piece of graph paper 25cm × 25cm
piece of iron-on interfacing 25cm × 25cm
all the other things you need for the vest (see p. 12)

You must sew the letter on to the front of the vest before you sew the front and back together.

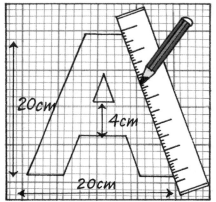

On the graph paper draw a letter about 20cm square, no part of it narrower than 4cm.

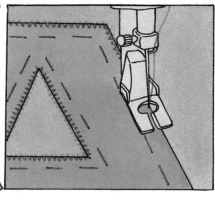

Cut out the letter and pin it on to the fabric. Draw round it and cut it out carefully.

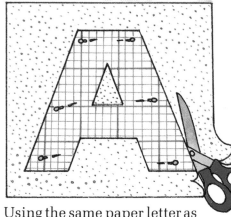

Using the same paper letter as your pattern, cut out an identical piece of interfacing.

Iron the interfacing * on to the wrong side of the fabric and tack the letter on to the vest.

Stitch round the letter, using a short, wide zigzag so that all the raw edges are covered.

Make the vest, following the method on pages 12 and 13.

14   * See page 28

Mini dress

You can adapt the vest pattern to make a mini dress. It is cut straight, so make sure that the finished chest measurement is the same size or bigger than your hip measurement.

You will need

1m of 115cm or 150cm wide jersey fabric
all the other things you need for the vest (see p. 12)

Sizes

To fit chest: 83/87cm
Finished size
chest: 85/90cm
length: 85cm

Method

Follow the basic vest pattern, but add 29cm to the length (this includes the hem).

Make up as for vest, following the method on pages 12 and 13.

Vest pattern

The seam allowance is 1cm throughout.

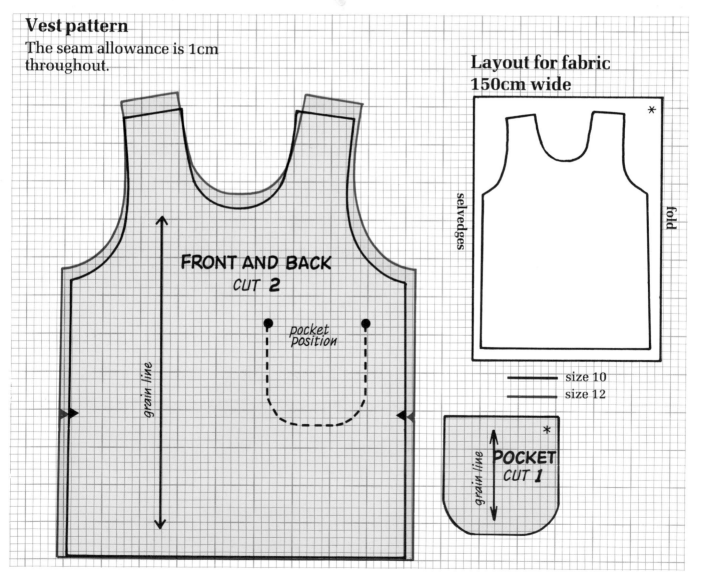

FRONT AND BACK
CUT 2

pocket
position

grain line

Layout for fabric 150cm wide

selvedges

fold

size 10
size 12

POCKET
CUT 1

grain line

* You can fit the pocket piece in to the right of the armhole when the fabric is unfolded.   **15**

Tee-shirt

You can make this simple tee shirt from almost any fabric (see below). You can make a short or long sleeved version and on page 18 you can find out how to make a mini tee-shirt.

Sizes

To fit chest: 83/87cm
Finished size
chest: 106/110cm
length: 56/58cm
long sleeve length: 47cm
short sleeve length: 15cm

Method

Make the tee-shirt pattern, following the chart on page 19 and cut it out. Then cut out the fabric.

Sewing jersey

If you are using jersey fabric to make the tee-shirt, remember to use zigzag stitch for all seams as for the vest on pages 12 and 13.

Suggested fabrics

Cotton jersey, stretch towelling, fine cotton, brushed cotton, Viyella, needlecord, satin.

Pocket

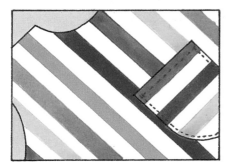

Hem top and sides of pockets as for vest pocket (see page 12). Tack in line with tailor tacks on front. Topstitch in place.

Shoulder seams

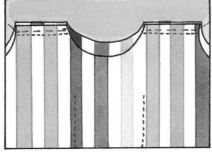

With right sides facing, pin the front and back of the tee-shirt together at shoulder seams and tack them in place.

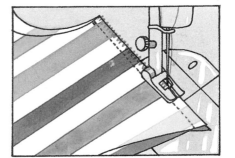

Take out pins and stitch seams. Neaten raw edges together, using zigzag stitch and press towards back of tee-shirt.

Sewing in sleeves

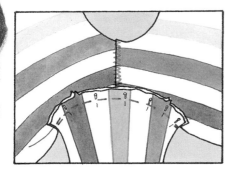

With right sides facing, pin sleeves into armholes, matching the notches. Tack in place; then take out pins.

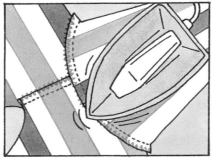

Stitch carefully, stretching fabric round lower armhole curves. Zigzag raw edges together and press inwards.

What is bias binding?

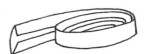

Bias binding is a kind of tape which is cut on the bias of the fabric (see page 45). This makes it stretchy and easy to bind round curved edges. It has a small, pressed hem along each edge.

Binding the neck

Cut a piece of bias binding 57/58cm long. With right sides facing, stitch the ends together to make a circle.

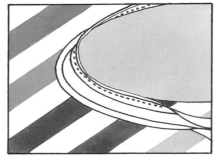

Pin right sides of binding to right side of neck so raw edges match. Tack. Stitch close to top fold in binding, as shown.

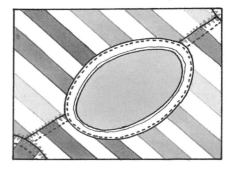

Press binding to wrong side of neck so seam is on the edge. Tack in place. Stitch close to fold in binding, as shown.

Underarm and side seams

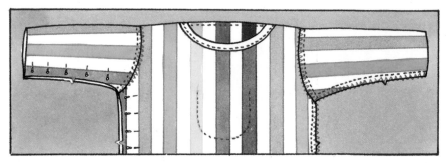

With right sides facing and matching notches, pin front to back at underarm sleeve and side seams.

Tack, then take out pins and stitch seams. Neaten raw edges together with zig zag stitch and press them towards back.

Hemming and finishing

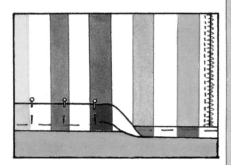

To make a hem, turn in 5mm round bottom of tee-shirt. Tack and press. Turn in another 2cm. Pin, tack and press. Stitch close to inner fold.

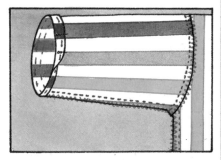

Hem sleeves in the same way, but make the second turnings 1cm deep. Turn tee-shirt the right way out and press*.

Mini Tee-shirt

You can adapt the tee-shirt pattern to make a mini version.

You will need

1m 60 of 92cm wide fabric
80cm of 115/150cm wide fabric
All the other things you need for the tee-shirt (see page 16).

Sizes

To fit chest: 83/87cm
Finished length: 39/41cm

Method

Make the pattern for short-sleeved tee-shirt, but cut along the mini tee-shirt cutting line. Make up as for tee-shirt **, following the method on pp. 17-18.

Appliqué Tee-shirt

Make an appliqué letter or number (see page 14) and stitch on to front of tee-shirt. Make up as for tee-shirt, following the method on pp. 17-18.

* Hem sleeves in the same way for short or long sleeves.
    ** The mini tee shirt has no pocket.

Tee-shirt pattern

Layout for fabric 115cm or 150cm wide

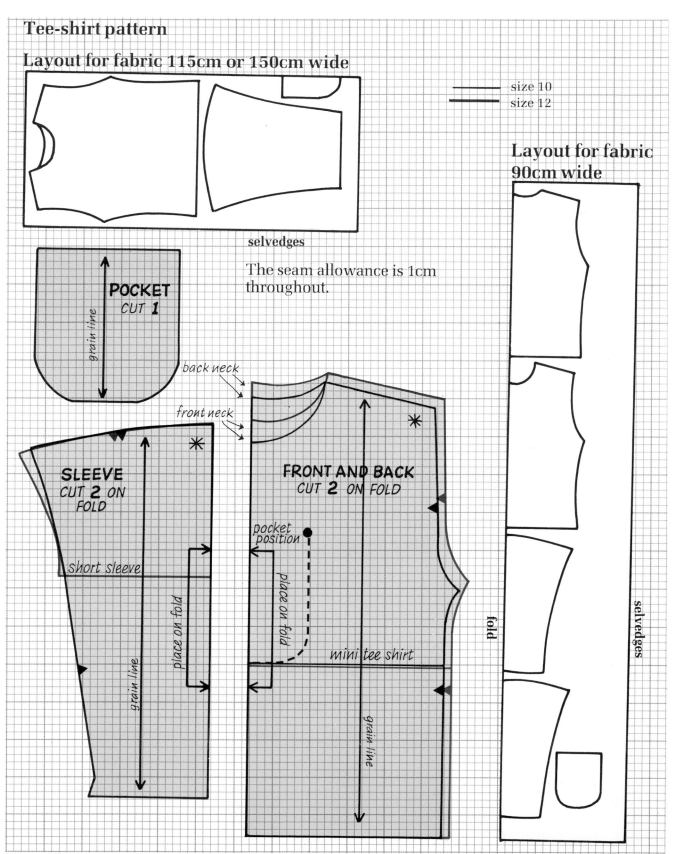

size 10
size 12

Layout for fabric 90cm wide

selvedges

The seam allowance is 1cm throughout.

POCKET
CUT 1

grain line

back neck

front neck

SLEEVE
CUT 2 ON FOLD

short sleeve

place on fold

grain line

FRONT AND BACK
CUT 2 ON FOLD

pocket position

place on fold

mini tee shirt

grain line

fold

selvedges

*If using fabric 115 or 150 cm wide, make pattern pieces for the complete front, back and sleeve by cutting them out on folded paper.

Sweatshirt

You will need
1 m 20/ 1 m 30 of
150 cm wide fabric
40 cm of matching
tubular knit ribbing at
least 60 cm wide (when flat)
ballpoint sewing needles
1 reel of matching
sewing thread

This sweatshirt is easier to make than you might think. It is the ribbing that makes it look professional and you can buy it from most department stores and fabric shops. If you cannot find the colour you want, buy white ribbing and dye it.

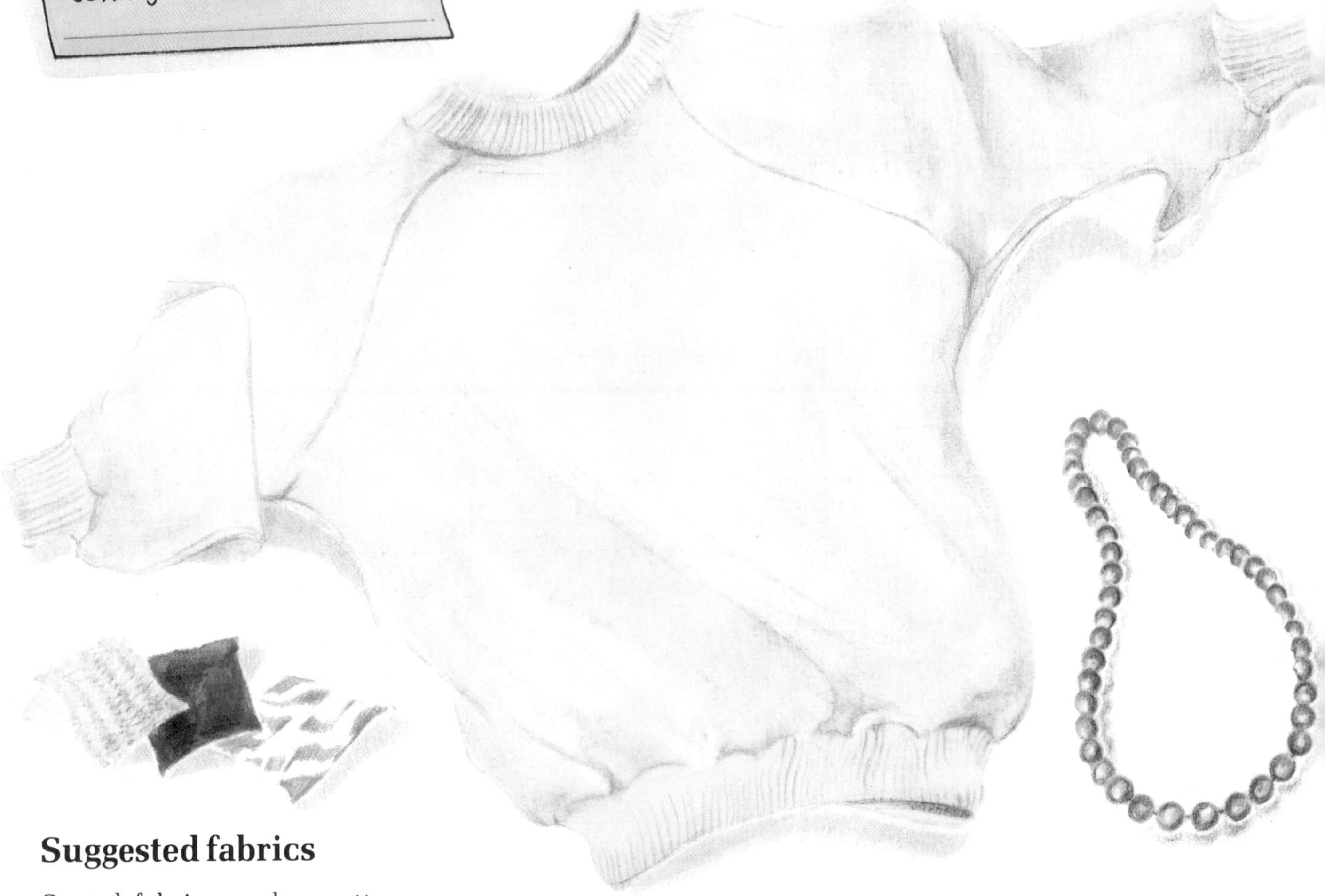

Suggested fabrics

Stretch fabrics, such as cotton or cotton/acrylic mix sweatshirt fabric, stretch towelling, heavy knit jersey*

Sizes

To fit chest: 83/87cm
Finished size
chest: 102/108cm
length: 59.5/62.5cm
underarm sleeve length: 46/47cm

Method

Make the sweatshirt pattern following the chart on page 37 and cut the following pieces from the sweatshirt ribbing:

Hipband: 2 pieces 15cm × 28cm
Cuffs: 2 pieces 15cm × 18cm
Neck: 1 piece 7.5cm × 43cm

*Remember to sew jersey fabric with zigzag stitch (see page 12).

Different kinds of sleeve

raglan sleeves   *set-in sleeves*

Raglan sleeves are different from 'set-in' sleeves. They join on to the neck, rather than the shoulder whereas set-in sleeves are stitched into the armhole of a garment.

Joining sleeves to armholes

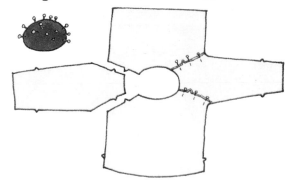

With right sides together, pin the raglan sleeves to the front and back of the sweatshirt along the shoulder seams, as shown. Tack in place.

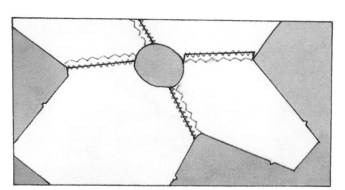

Stitch with a medium, narrow zigzag stitch (use throughout for stitching seams). Neaten raw edges together with a short, wide zigzag stitch and press towards body of sweatshirt.

Underarm and side seams

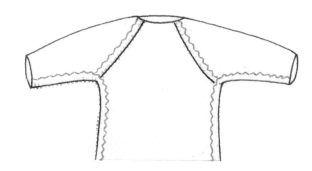

Pin side seams and underarm sleeve seams together. Tack. Stitch, stretching fabric gently round the underarm curves. Neaten raw edges together and press towards back.

Hipband

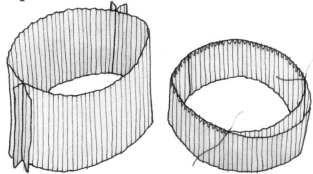

With right sides of hipband ribbing facing, tack side seams. Stitch, turning right sides out, and fold in half lengthwise to make a tube. Zigzag stitch raw edges together loosely.

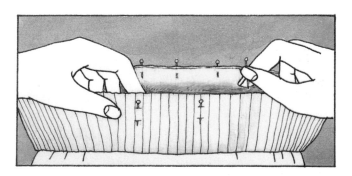

Place right side of the ribbing tube against right side of the sweatshirt, matching side seams, and pin evenly around the hem, stretching the ribbing to fit. Tack in place.

Cuffs

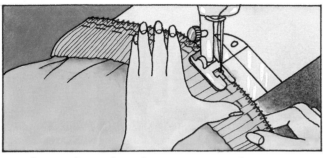

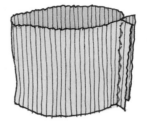

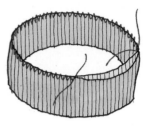

Stitch 1cm from the edge, using a medium, narrow zigzag setting, and stretching the ribbing as you stitch. Zigzag stitch the raw edges together as before.

Fold each cuff in half widthwise and stitch the short ends together with right sides facing. Turn right sides out and fold lengthwise as for hipband. Tack. Zigzag raw edges together.

Short sleeved sweatshirt

This short-sleeved sweatshirt makes a cool and casual summer top.

You will need

1m/1m 10 of 150cm wide fabric
40cm of ribbing
all the other things you need for the sweatshirt (see page 20)

Method

When making your pattern, cut off sleeves at short sleeve line. Cut 2 cuff ribs 8cm × 26cm. Make up cuff and stitch on to sleeve as for sweatshirt (see pp. 20 and 21).

Loose, baggy top

You can adapt the pattern to make this top without ribbing. Instead of sewing ribbing to the cuffs, neck and hipband, neatly stitch along the raw edges using a short, wide zigzag stitch. The fabric will curl up with wear and cover the stitching.

loose, baggy top

short sleeved sweatshirt

Neckband

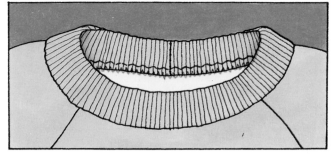

Pin cuffs to right sides of sleeves, as shown. Match seams and stretch ribbing to fit. Tack and stitch. Zigzag raw edges together to neaten them.

Make ribbing into tube as for cuffs. Match seam to centre back of sweatshirt and pin ribbing evenly around neck. Tack, stitch and neaten as before, then press lightly.

Sweatshirt pattern

The seam allowance is 1cm throughout.

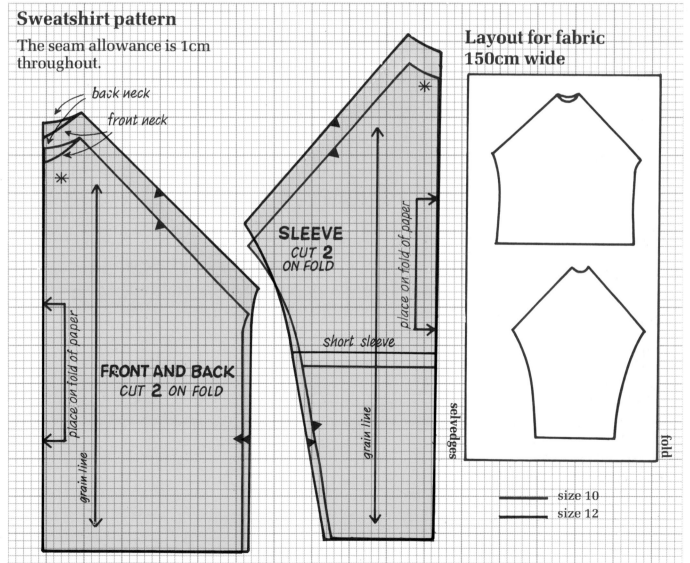

back neck

front neck

SLEEVE
CUT **2**
ON FOLD

place on fold of paper

short sleeve

grain line

FRONT AND BACK
CUT **2** ON FOLD

place on fold of paper

grain line

Layout for fabric 150cm wide

selvedges

fold

size 10
size 12

*Make pattern pieces for the complete back, front and sleeve by cutting them on folded paper.

Jeans

You will need

2 m 80 of 90 cm wide fabric **OR**

2 m 40 of 115 cm wide fabric **OR**

1 m 50 of 150 cm wide fabric

1 reel of matching Sewing Thread

1 reel of contrasting thread (for topstitching)

70 cm of 3 cm wide elastic

large safety pin

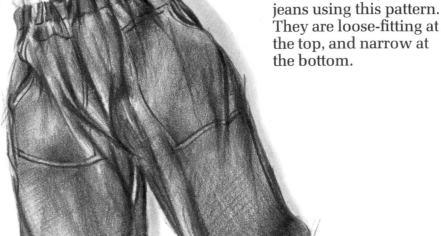

You can make your own jeans using this pattern. They are loose-fitting at the top, and narrow at the bottom.

Suggested fabrics

Cottons: poplin, drill, crinkle cotton, denim, needlecord.

Sizes

To fit hips: 88/92cm
waist: 64/74cm
Finished size
hips: 96/102cm
length: 102/106cm
inside leg length: 73/75cm

Method

Make the pattern following the chart on pages 26 and 27 and cut it out. Then cut out the fabric.

How to double topstitch seams

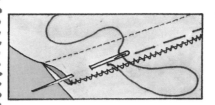 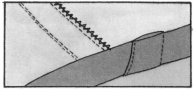

On the wrong side of the garment, tack down the neatened edge of the seam allowance through all layers of fabric. Then turn garment the right way out.

Do two lines of topstitching— one next to the seam, just inside the seam allowance, and the other about 6mm away (next to zigzag edge on wrong side of fabric).

Crutch seams

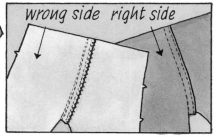

With right sides facing, tack two trouser fronts together along the crutch seam (curved seam between top of inside leg and waist). Stitch.

Neaten raw edges together. Press to right of seam. Double topstitch (see opposite page). Do the back crutch seam in the same way.

Back pockets

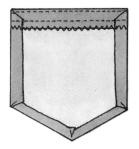

Neaten top edges of back pockets. Press 1.5cm to wrong side. Double topstitch. Press 1cm to wrong side round three remaining edges.

Front pockets

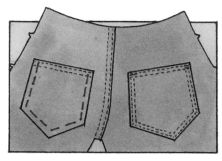

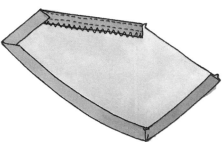

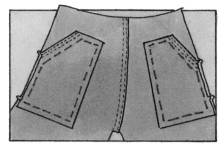

Line pockets up with tacks on back of trousers. Tack. Double topstitch round unstitched sides of pockets. Leave the tops open.

Neaten sloping edges of front pockets, as for tops of back pockets. Turn in 1cm to wrong side at top, bottom and long side of front pockets. Press.

Tack the pockets in line with tailor tacks on front of trousers, matching notches so that raw edges of pockets match side edges of trousers.

Side seams

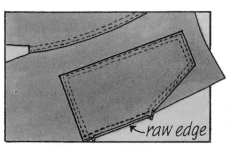

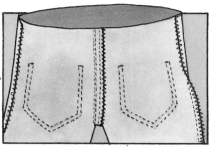

Double topstitch round top, long side and bottom of pockets. Stitch raw edges of pockets to edges of trousers, 5mm in.

With right sides facing, tack front to back of trousers at side seams. Stitch. Neaten seams and press towards back. Double topstitch.

Inside leg seams

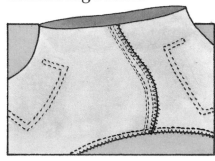

With right sides of fabric facing, tack inside leg seams. Stitch. Neaten seams together and press them towards the back of trousers.

What is a casing?

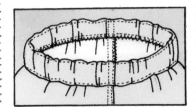

A casing is a tube of fabric threaded with elastic or cord. It makes a comfortable waistband which you can adjust to fit.

Waistband

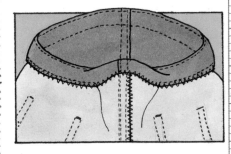

Zig zag waist edge of trousers and turn in 5cm. Press. Tack. Topstitch close to fold and again, 3.5cm lower down, leaving a 4cm gap at back seam.

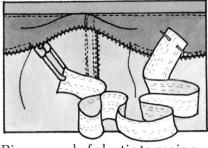

Pin one end of elastic to casing. Thread other end through with a big safety pin. Pin both ends together. Try on trousers and adjust elastic to fit.

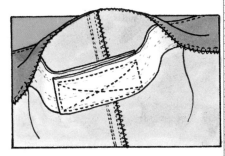

Stitch ends of elastic together being careful not to stitch it to casing at same time. Trim spare elastic 1cm from stitching. Topstitch 4cm gap in casing.

Hems

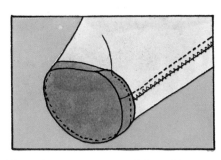

Turn in 5mm on each leg. Press. Turn in another 1cm to hide raw edges. Press and tack. Topstitch. Roll up hems to the length you want.

Jeans pattern

Layout for fabric 150cm wide

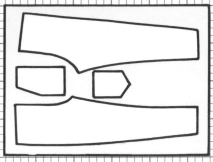

fold

The seam allowance is 1cm throughout.

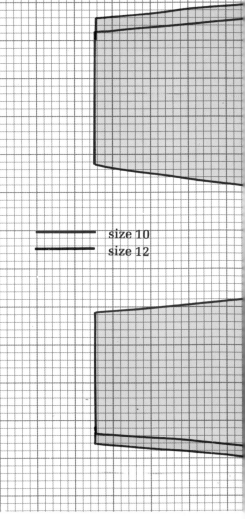

—————— size 10
—————— size 12

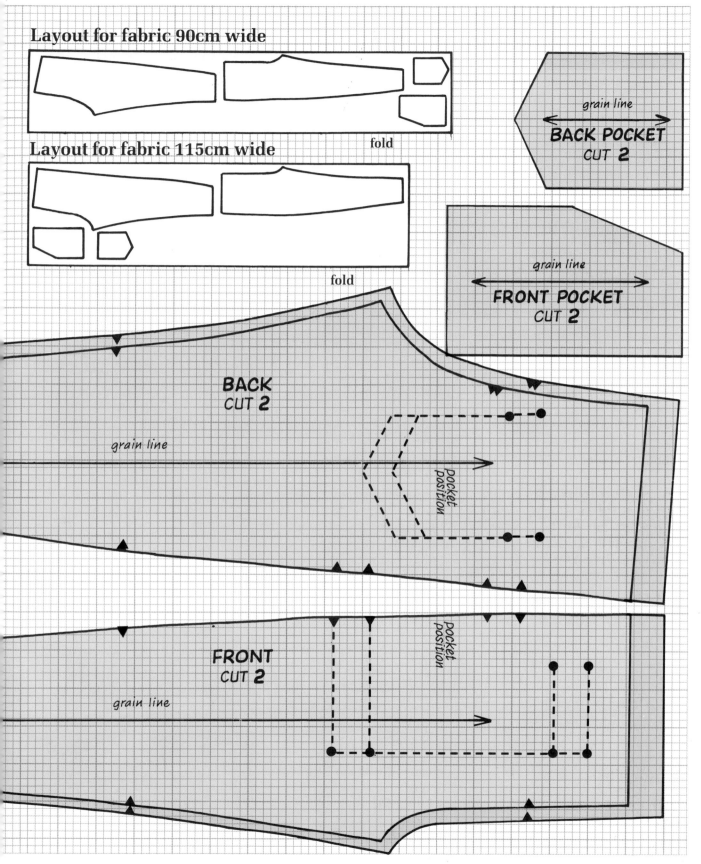

Layout for fabric 90cm wide

fold

Layout for fabric 115cm wide

fold

grain line

BACK POCKET
CUT **2**

grain line

FRONT POCKET
CUT **2**

BACK
CUT **2**

grain line

pocket position

FRONT
CUT **2**

grain line

pocket position

Gathered skirt

You will need:
2 m 10 of 115 cm wide fabric
1 reel of matching thread
20 cm zip fastener
1 button, 1 cm across
10 cm of medium weight iron-on interfacing
tailor's chalk

You do not need a pattern for this skirt. It is just made from two rectangles of fabric, a waistband and two pockets.

Sizes

To fit waist: 64/67cm
Finished size
length (including waistband): 84cm
width round hem: 224cm

Suggested fabrics

Cotton poplin, lawn, madras, seersucker, brushed cotton, Viyella, fine needlecord.

Method

Cut out the following widths of fabric, as shown in the pattern layout on p. 31.

2 widths 86cm deep for skirt
1 waistband, 10cm × 66/71cm
2 pockets, 21cm × 27cm

Interfacing

Cut 1 strip for the waistband, 5cm × 66/71cm.
Cut 2 strips 3cm × 21cm for the tops of the pockets.

What is interfacing?

Interfacing is a special fabric you attach to the wrong side of fabric you want to stiffen. It comes in different weights. The iron-on kind is the easiest to use.

Attaching interfacing

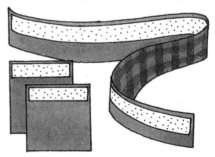

Iron the wrong side of the interfacing on to the wrong side of the tops of the pockets and lengthways on to one half of the waistband.

Pockets

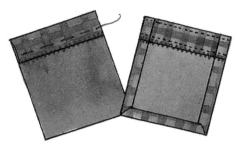

Zigzag stitch top edges of pockets and turn in 3cm hems. Tack, press and stitch twice, as shown. Press 1cm hems around other 3 sides of pockets.

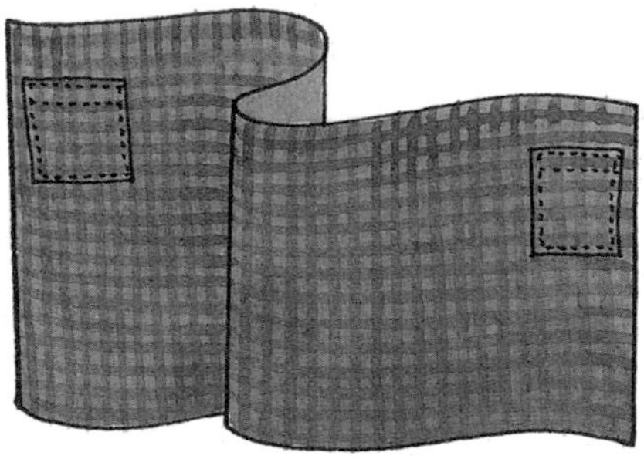

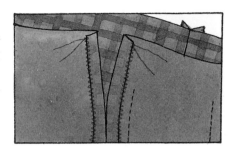

Tack pockets on to skirt front, 9cm below top edge and 3cm in from side edges. Topstitch around 3 sides of pockets about 2mm in from the edges.

Side seams

Side seams illustration at top right.

With right sides of skirt together, tack side seams. Leave a 21cm gap at top of left seam for zip. Stitch. Neaten seams with zigzag and press open.

Using a zip foot

A zip foot has a notch on each side so that you can stitch to the right or the left of the zip. Stitch both sides of the zip from the base upwards.

Stitch the right side of the zip first, with the zip foot to the left of the needle. Move the foot to the right of the needle to stitch the left side of the zip.

Zip

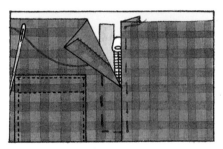

With skirt right sides out, put zip in opening, 1.5cm from top of skirt. Tack right side of zip so fabric almost meets teeth and left side so fabric covers teeth.

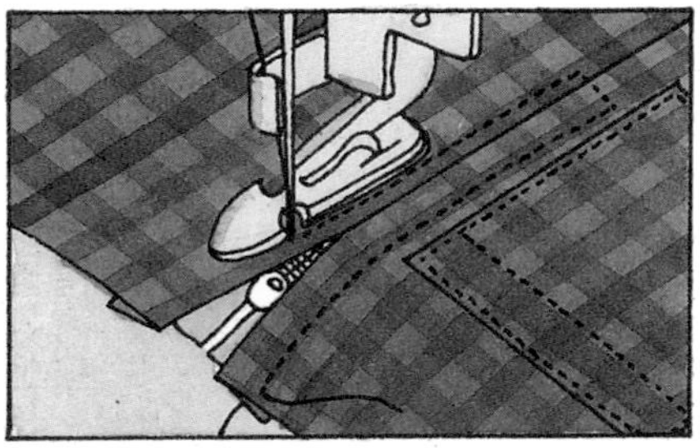

Using a zip foot, stitch zip into opening so that stitching comes close to edge of pocket on front of skirt and close to fold on back of skirt.

Gathers

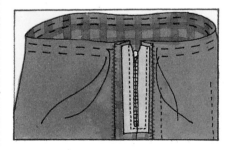

Set the machine to a long stitch length. Stitch twice round the top of the skirt, 5mm and 1.5cm below top edge. Leave long threads at beginning and end.

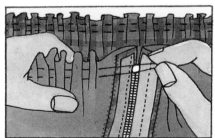

Gently pull ends of both threads to gather waist until it measures 61/66cm (each side should measure half this). Tie ends of threads together.

Waistband

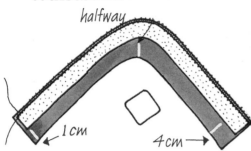

Zigzag along interfaced edge of waistband. Measure 1cm in from left end, 4cm from right end and halfway between the two and mark with chalk.

With right sides together, pin waistband to skirt, lining up chalk marks, as shown. Adjust gathers evenly between marks. Tack in place.

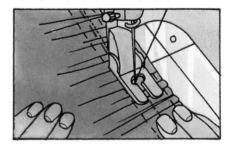

Stitch waistband to skirt with a 1cm seam allowance. Stitch between the rows of gathering. Take out the lower row of gathering stitches.

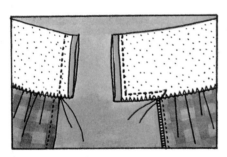

Fold waistband in half, right sides together, and tack each end so it is square. Stitch 1cm in. At end with overlap, stitch along lower edge as far as zip.

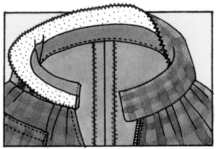

Trim corners of waistband and turn right way out. Ease out corners so you have neat, square edges. Press waistband in half to finished depth of 4cm.

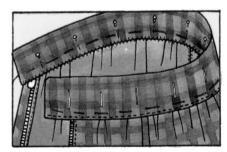

Pin neatened edge of waistband to wrong side of skirt, covering raw edges. Tack in place so it lies smoothly. Stitch along right side, close to seam.

Hem

Finishing

Try on skirt. Ask a friend to pin up hem to the length you want. For a 5cm hem*, turn up and press 5mm to wrong side. Turn up a further 4.5cm and tack.

Hem neatly by hand (see page 43), making sure that the stitches do not show on the right side and that the stitching does not pucker.

Handsew or machine a 1cm horizontal buttonhole on front of waistband 1cm in from edge (see opposite). Sew a button on to overlapping flap.

* Whatever depth you want the hem to be, remember to allow 5mm for the first turning.

Machine stitched buttonholes

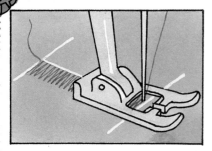

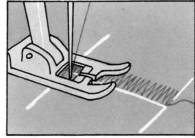

Attach buttonhole foot*. Mark buttonhole position. With short, wide zigzag work down one side of buttonhole on right side of garment.

When you reach end marker, lift foot and turn fabric. Set stitch width to its widest and make a few stitches the width of whole buttonhole.

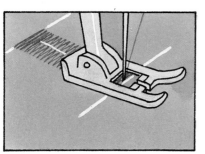

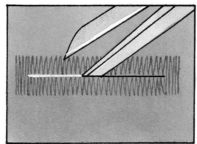

Re-set stitch width to its previous position. Stitch other side of buttonhole. Make a few stitches the width of buttonhole at end.

Tie loose threads together at back. Snip down middle of buttonhole, being careful not to cut any stitches.

Sewing on buttons

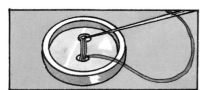

Sew through button

With a double length of knotted thread, stitch through button and fabric, keeping a small gap in between. Fasten off on wrong side.

Shank button

Holding button at right angles to fabric, stitch through the hole in the shank and through the fabric. Fasten off securely.

* Look in your machine handbook to find out how.

Fabric layout for skirt

FRONT
CUT 1 ON FOLD

BACK
CUT 1 ON FOLD

fold

WAISTBAND
CUT 1 ON FOLD

POCKET
CUT 2

Layout for fabric 115cm or 150cm wide

Baggy shirt

This loose-fitting shirt can look smart or casual, depending on the fabric you make it from. It is suitable for boys or girls.

Suggested fabrics

Fine cottons, lawn, voile, poplin, seersucker, brushed cotton, viyella.

Sizes

To fit chest: 83/87cm
Finished size chest: 118/122cm
back length: 72/74cm
(excluding collar)
underarm sleeve: 43/45cm
collar size: 36/39cm

Interfacing

From the interfacing, cut a collar piece, a neckband piece and 2 cuff pieces (half the width of the cuff). Trim off seam allowances (1cm). Cut a strip 3cm × 63/64cm for the buttonband.

Method

Make the shirt pattern, following the chart on pp. 36 and 37 and cut it out. Then cut out the fabric.

Attaching interfacing

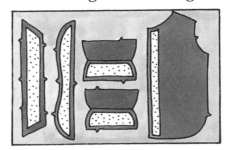

Iron interfacing on to wrong side of fabric with warm iron. Iron buttonband strip 5mm from edge on wrong side of right*front.

* Left front for boy's shirt.

Pleats

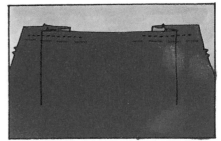

On back of shirt fold 2 pleats towards armholes, matching notches. Tack in place. Stitch across pleats close to top edge, to hold them in place.

What is a facing?

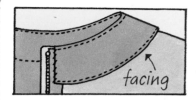

A facing is used to line and strengthen edges, such as necklines, armholes and yokes. It is usually made of the same fabric as the garment.

Trimming a seam allowance

Some seams are too bulky, even with a 1cm seam allowance (for example, on collars, yokes and curved seams). Carefully trim these seams to about 5mm.

Yoke

With right sides together and matching notches, pin shirt yoke to back and tack it in place. Stitch, making sure the pleats lie flat.

Pin right side of yoke facing to wrong side of back. Tack in place, then stitch along the seamline you made when stitching yoke to back.

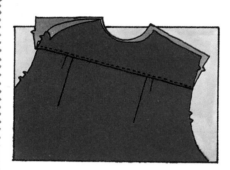

Trim seam allowance (see left) and fold yoke pieces upwards. Press together, as shown. Topstitch, just above the seamline.

Pocket

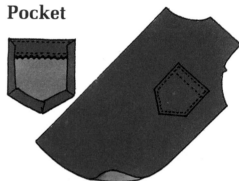

Neaten and turn in 3cm at top of pocket. Press. Stitch twice, as shown. Press 5mm turnings round rest of pocket and tack in place on shirt front. Topstitch.

Shoulder seams

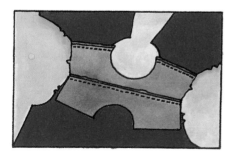

Match right side of yoke facing to wrong side of shirt front at shoulder seams. Tack. Stitch. Trim seams and press them towards yoke.

Lay shirt flat on table. Pin yoke pieces together. Turn under 1cm on yoke shoulders. Tack over raw edges, as shown. Topstitch close to folds.

Right front

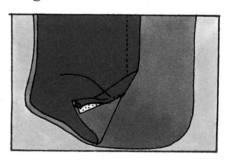

Turn in 5mm along long edge of right front*. Press. Stitch close to fold. Turn in another 3.5cm and press. Tack. Topstitch close to fold.

* Reverse instructions for the right and left fronts for a boy's shirt.

Left front

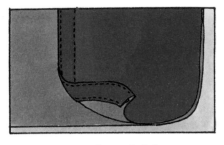

Turn in 4cm along left front. Tack. Press. Topstitch close to fold. Press 1cm to wrong side along raw edge. Stitch and press.

Sleeves

With right sides of fabric facing, pin sleeves into armholes, matching notches. Tack. Stitch, stretching fabric gently round curves.

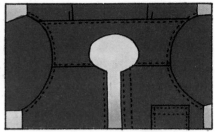

Neaten raw edges together with zig zag stitch. Press neatened edges towards body of shirt. Topstitch on body side of seamline.

Collar

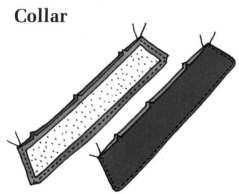

With right sides facing, tack collar pieces together round 3 sides. Stitch, clip corners and trim seam. Turn right way out. Topstitch as shown.

With right sides facing, tack edges of neckband to collar, as shown, matching notches. Stitch. Trim seam. Turn neckband right way out. Press.

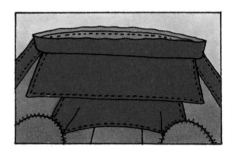

Tack inside edge of neckband to wrong side of neck edge of shirt, as shown, matching notches. Stitch neckband in place and trim seam allowance.

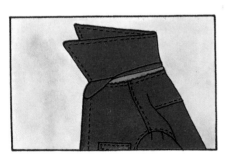

Press seam towards neckband. Press 1cm turning to wrong side along free edge of neckband. Turn it to right side of shirt.

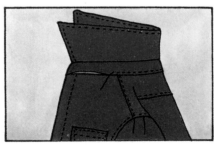

Tack down free edge of neckband, so it covers raw edge on right side of shirt. Topstitch around side and bottom edges of neckband and press.

Side seams

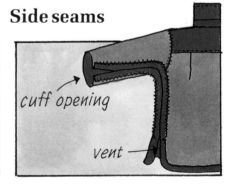

With right sides facing, tack sleeve and side seams, matching notches. Stitch from notch at sleeve opening to hem notch. Neaten raw edges apart.

Sleeve openings

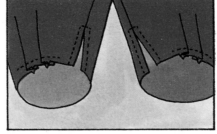

Cuffs

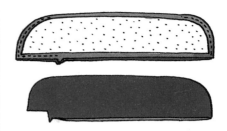

Tack down seam allowance at sleeve opening. Stitch around opening, about 5mm in, up one side, flat across top, and down other side.

Matching notches, fold two pleats towards back of shirt on each sleeve. Tack down and stitch across tops of pleats to hold them in place.

Fold cuffs as shown, right sides together. Tack round curved edge as far as notch. Stitch. Trim seam and clip corners. Turn right way out. Press.

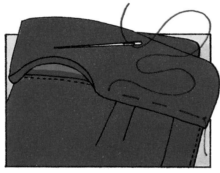

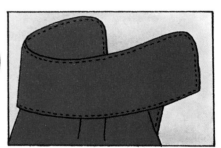

Tack inside of cuff to sleeve, with right side of cuff facing wrong side of sleeve. Trim seam and press raw edge towards sleeve.

Turn in 1cm along free edge of cuff and press. Turn free edge of cuff over to right side of sleeve and tack it over raw edges of seam.

On the right side topstitch carefully all the way around each cuff, being careful not to pucker the fabric as you do so.

Hem

Finishing

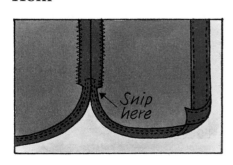

Turn in 5mm around bottom of shirt. Press and stitch. Turn in another 5mm to cover raw edges. Press and stitch as for sleeve openings.

Make 6 buttonholes,* 1.25cm wide, down right** front, 7.5 mm from edge. Make top one in neckband, next one 3cm below and space the rest 10cm apart.

Make a buttonhole in each cuff, 1cm from left edge. Stitch buttons under buttonholes on left** front of shirt and halfway down each cuff overlap.

* See page 31 for machine stitched buttonholes
** Reverse instructions for the right and left fronts for a boy's shirt.

Baggy shirt pattern

Layout for fabric 115cm wide

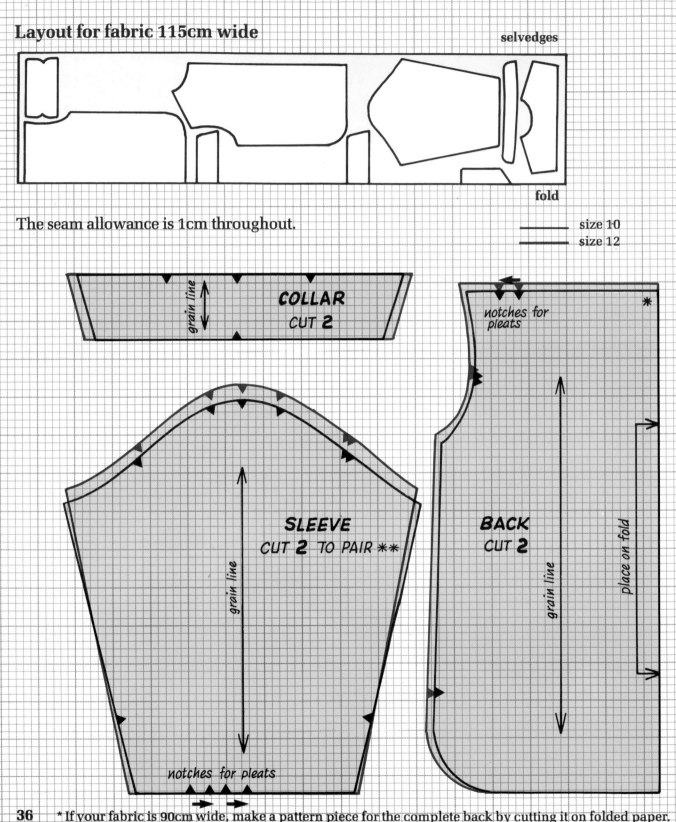

selvedges

fold

The seam allowance is 1cm throughout.

———— size 10
———— size 12

COLLAR
CUT **2**

grain line

notches for pleats

SLEEVE
CUT **2** TO PAIR **

grain line

notches for pleats

BACK
CUT **2**

grain line

place on fold

*

* If your fabric is 90cm wide, make a pattern piece for the complete back by cutting it on folded paper.

Layout for fabric 90cm wide

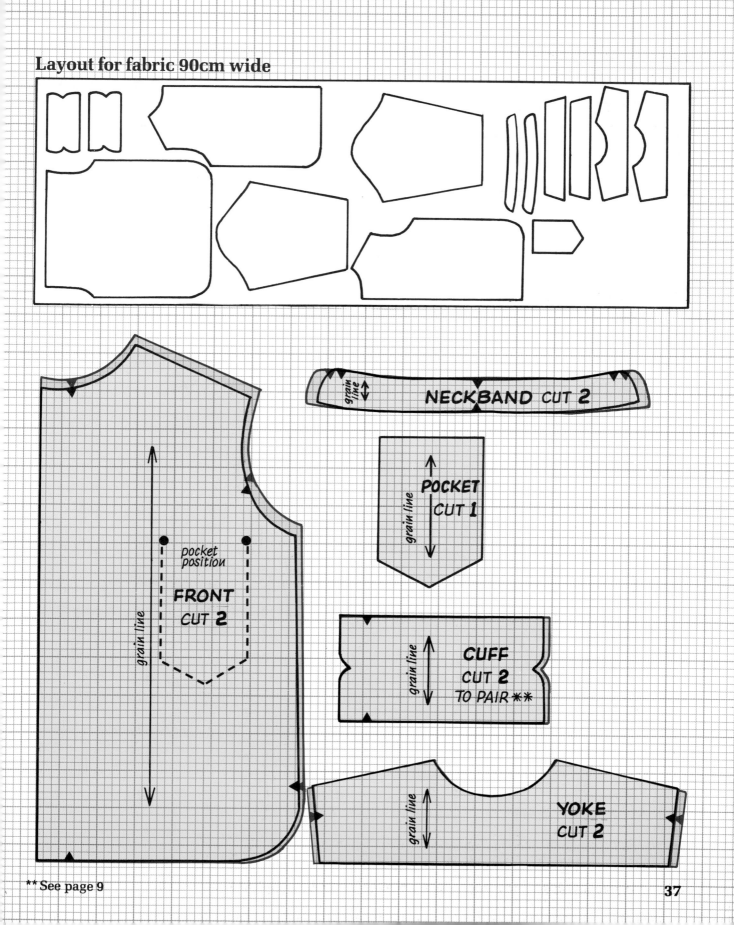

NECKBAND CUT 2

grain line

POCKET CUT 1

grain line

CUFF CUT 2 TO PAIR **

grain line

FRONT CUT 2

pocket position

grain line

YOKE CUT 2

grain line

Jumpsuit

This loose-fitting jumpsuit fits sizes 10 and 12.

Sizes

To fit chest: 83/87cm
Finished size
Length: 147cm
Inside leg length: 73cm
Back body length: 80cm
Chest: 112cm
Underarm sleeve length: 43cm

Suggested fabrics

Fine cottons, seersucker, crinkle cotton, poplin, brushed cotton, Viyella

Method

Make the pattern, following the chart on pages 40 and 41 and cut out. Then cut out the fabric.

Centre back seam

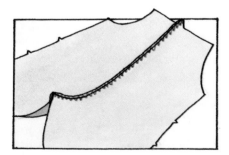

With right sides together, tack 2 back pieces together. Stitch, stretching fabric around the curve, neaten raw edges together and press to one side.

Centre front seam

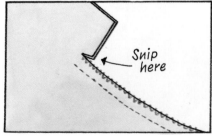

Tack centre front seam, with right sides together. Stitch. Snip into corner at top of seam. Neaten raw edges together and press to one side.

Yoke

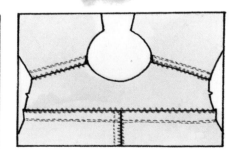

Stitch yoke to back, right sides together. Neaten raw edges together and press upwards. Topstitch. Stitch front shoulder and yoke seams in same way.

Pockets

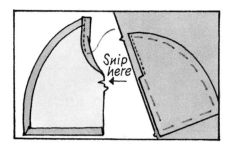

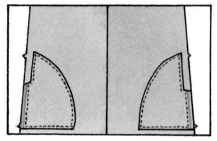

Turn in 1cm above notch on pocket edge. Press. Stitch 5mm in. Turn in 1cm along curved and bottom edges. Press. Tack to front, in line with notches.

Topstitch pockets round curves and bottom edges. Stitch raw edges of pockets to side edges of jumpsuit about 5mm in.

Sleeves and body seams

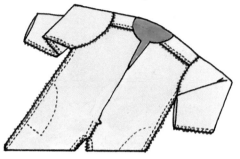

Sew in sleeves as for tee-shirt*. Tack underarm and side seams. Stitch. Neaten seams and press towards back. Stitch inside leg seams in the same way.

Facing

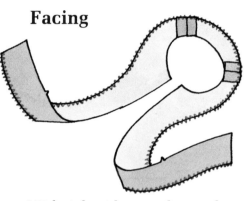

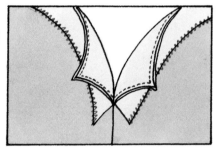

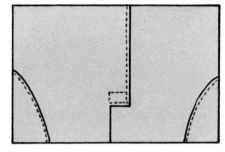

With right sides together, tack front facing to back neck facing at shoulder seams. Stitch. Press seams open. Zigzag round outside edge of facing.

Tack facing to neck and front openings so lower edge comes 1cm below front openings. Stitch round facing and across lower edge as far as centre front.

Trim seam, clip corners and turn right way out. Press. Topstitch, as shown. Lap right front over left at bottom of opening and topstitch a square.

Finishing

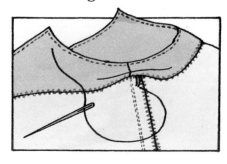

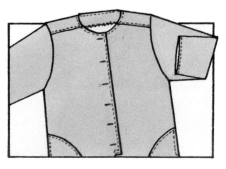

Lightly oversew facings to shoulder seams by hand**. Hem sleeves and legs, making first turning 5mm and second one 1cm. Topstitch.

Make 6 buttonholes◆ 1.5cm wide on right front, 7.5mm in from edge: top one 1.25cm below neck and five more spaced 10cm apart below that.

Stitch buttons under buttonholes on left front. Try on jumpsuit. Roll up sleeves and hems to right length. Oversew lightly at seams.

* See page 17   ** See page 42   ◆ See page 31 for machine stitched buttonholes

Jumpsuit pattern (one size)

Layout for fabric 90cm wide

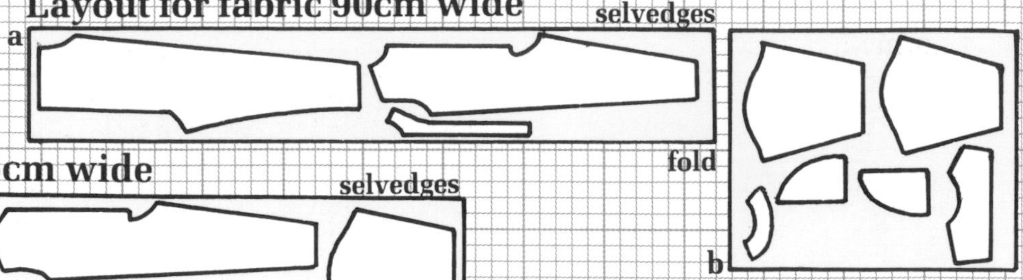
selvedges
a
fold
b

Layout for fabric 115cm wide

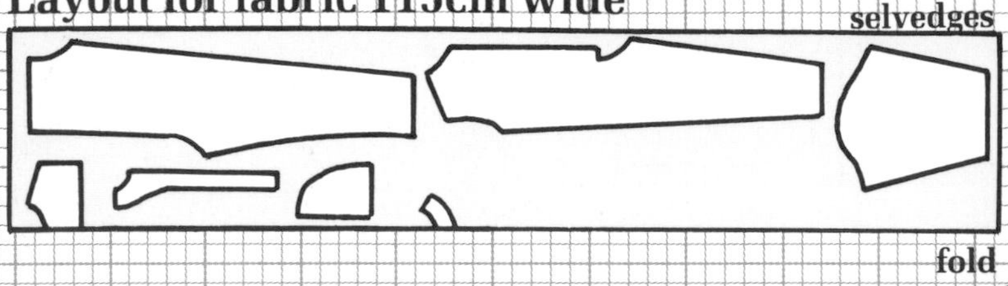
selvedges
fold

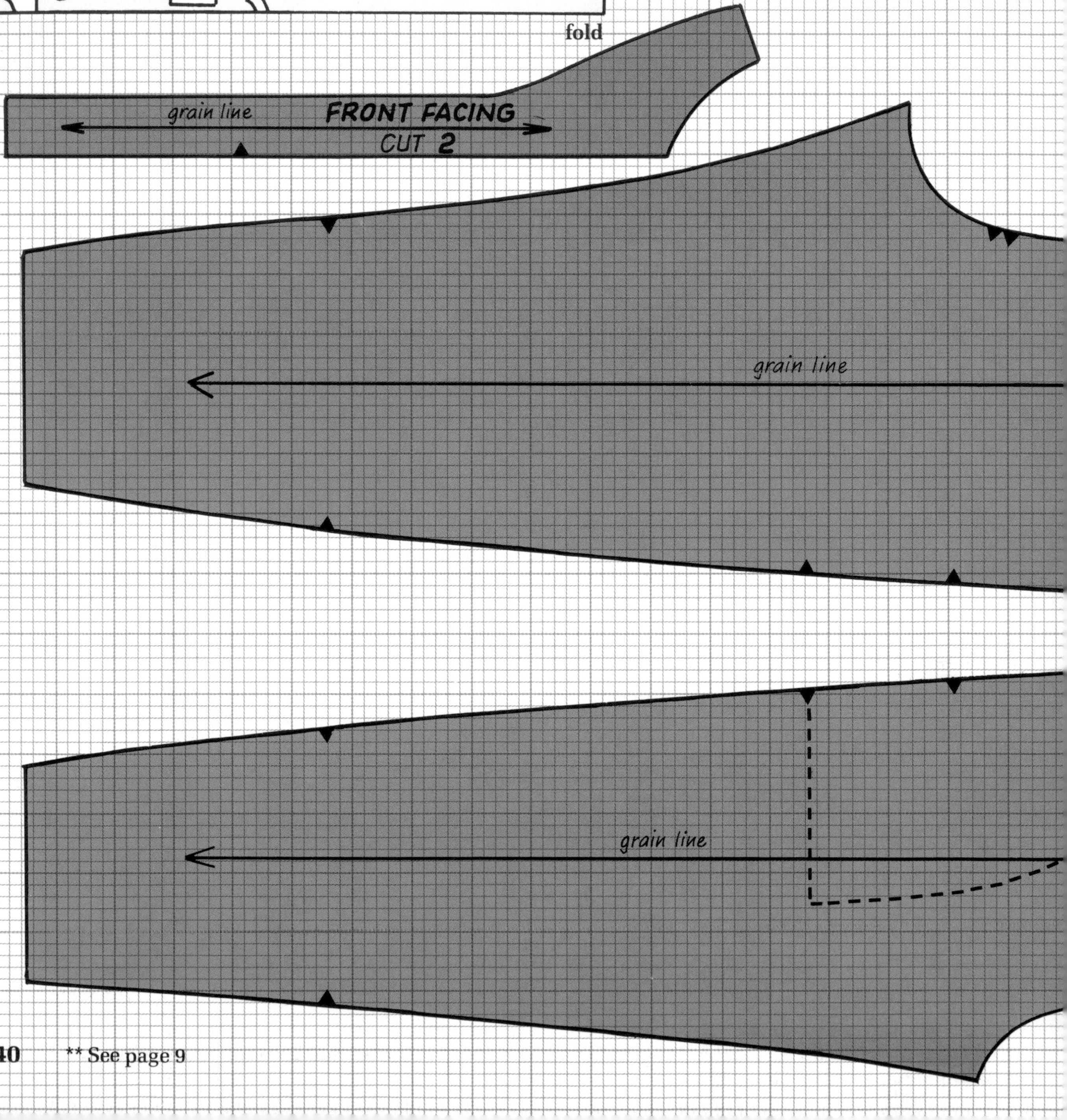
grain line
FRONT FACING
CUT 2
grain line
grain line

 ** See page 9

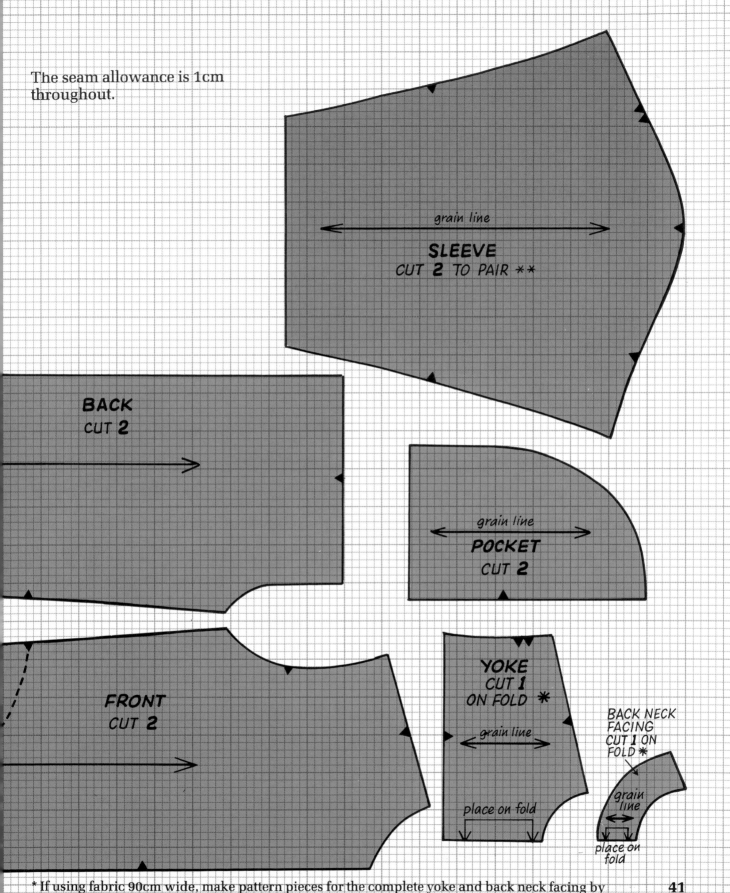

The seam allowance is 1cm throughout.

SLEEVE
CUT **2** TO PAIR * *

grain line

BACK
CUT **2**

POCKET
CUT **2**

grain line

FRONT
CUT **2**

YOKE
CUT **1**
ON FOLD *

grain line

place on fold

BACK NECK FACING
CUT **1** ON FOLD *

grain line

place on fold

* If using fabric 90cm wide, make pattern pieces for the complete yoke and back neck facing by cutting them out on folded paper.

Basic hand sewing

Nearly everything you make needs some kind of hand sewing. It is used for tacking, neatening and finishing off clothes.

Here you can find out how to do some of the most useful stitches. Practise them on scraps of fabric before you start sewing.

Needles

The most useful general needles for hand sewing are called Sharps. Use fine needles for delicate fabrics and thicker ones for the heavier fabrics.

Thread

Use the same thread as you use for machining (see page 44). You can buy special thread for tacking.

Scissors

You will need a small pair of sharp scissors.

Things to remember

Start off your sewing on the wrong side of the fabric, by tying a knot in the end of the thread or by making a few tiny stitches on top of each other.

Try to make all the stitches the same size and do not pull the thread too tightly.

Tack everything before you hand sew it. Take the tacking out when you have finished and press your sewing.

Do not use too long a piece of thread for handsewing, or it will get knots in it.

Tacking

Tacking is big stitches. You tack things to hold them in position while you stitch them properly, then take the tacking out when you have finished.

For areas which need to be held more securely, such as curves, make the stitches smaller and sew them closer together.

Oversewing

If your machine does not have a zigzag stitch, oversew raw edges by hand to stop them from fraying.

Do not pull the thread too tightly or the edge of the fabric will pucker.

If the fabric is likely to fray badly, sew the stitches closer together.

Making a hem

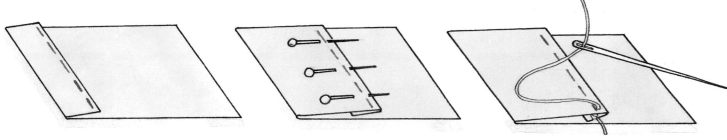

Turn the edge of the fabric in about 5mm. Tack it in place and press it.

Make a second turning the depth you want the hem. Pin and tack. Remove pins. Press.

Start with your knot or overstitching on the wrong side of the fabric.

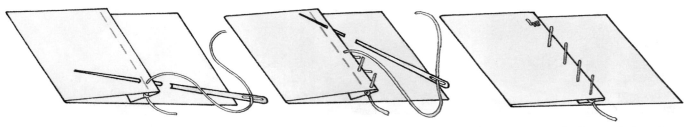

Catch two threads of the single layer of fabric and a stitch in the hem with the needle, as shown.

Carry on, keeping the stitches even. Do not pull the threads too tight.

When you reach the end, finish off with several small stitches on top of each other.

Making a buttonhole

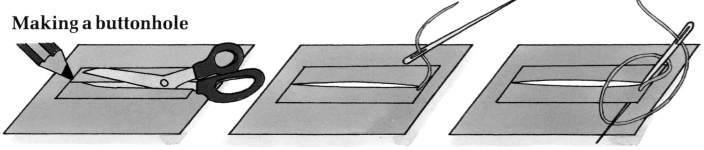

Draw a pencil rectangle on the fabric the width you want the buttonhole to be. Draw a line half-way across and slit it.

Work from right to left. Secure the thread with backstitch on the wrong side and bring the needle through to the right side.

Put the needle through the slit and bring it up on the pencil line. Loop the thread round it. Pull it through to make a knot.

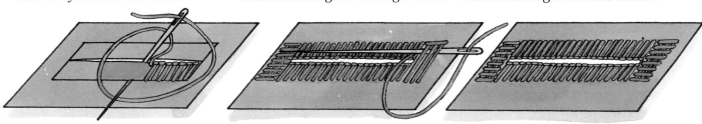

Start the second stitch close to the first one. Continue until you reach the end of the buttonhole.

Make 3 stitches the width of the whole buttonhole, as shown, then work the smaller stitches crosswise over the top.

Stitch the other side of the buttonhole. Neaten the end as before. Finish off with backstitch on the wrong side.

Choosing fabric and thread

There is a vast choice of different fabrics. You can buy them from department stores or fabric shops. Market stalls are good places to look too, but make sure you know what kind of fabric you are buying.

If you are just beginning to make clothes, choose firm, light to medium weight fabrics to start with as they are easiest to sew. Here you can find out about the main types of fabric.

Natural fabrics

Cotton

Light to medium weight. Different types, such as poplin (thick and crisp), lawn (fine) and voile (very fine). Easy to sew, but creases.

Wool

Warm and does not crease much. Use fine wool to make dresses, medium weight wool to make skirts and the heavier wools to make coats and jackets.

Corduroy

Thick, ribbed and has a 'pile' (see 'What is a nap?').

Viyella

Wool and cotton mixture. Warm. Good for shirts and dresses.

Jersey

Stretchy. Can be made of cotton or wool. Cotton jersey is good for sweatshirts and sportswear. Wool jersey is expensive and is used mainly for winter dresses.

Silk

Fine and expensive. Can be hard to sew because it is slippery. Used for party clothes.

Linen

Medium-weight, comfortable to wear. Expensive and creases easily. Used for summer clothes.

Threads

Choose thread to match the fabric you are sewing. Use cotton thread with natural fabrics, silk thread with silk and synthetic thread with man-made fabrics and jersey.

Buy thread a shade darker than your fabric as it looks lighter when you sew it.

You can buy special fine thread for tacking.

What are synthetics?

Synthetics are man-made fibres such as polyester, acrylic and nylon. They are cheaper than natural fabrics. You can buy mixtures of synthetic and natural fabrics which are easy to sew and wash.

Things you should know

Most fabrics are either knitted or woven. Knitted fabric, or jersey, is stretchy; woven fabric is firmer. The threads that run down it are called warp threads. Those that run from side to side are called weft threads. If you pull the fabric diagonally, you will find the 'bias'. This is the direction with most stretch.

The smooth, warp edges of woven fabrics are called selvedges.

What is a nap?

Some fabric has a 'pile' or furry surface, which feels smooth if you stroke it one way, but rough if you stroke it the other way. This is called a 'nap'. See page 9 to find out how to cut out napped fabric.

Fabrics such as taffeta which reflect the light in different ways also have a nap.

Patterned fabric

Some patterns are woven or knitted into the fabric, others are printed on. If a pattern is printed, the fabric has a right and wrong side. The pattern is fainter on the wrong side.

If your pattern goes in only one direction, treat it as though it has a nap (see above).

Things to remember

Take your pattern with you when buying fabric. Fabric comes in different widths and the pattern tells you how much of a width you need. It also suggests suitable fabrics for the garments you are making.

Make sure you choose the right type and weight of fabric for the time of year.

Look for fabrics which are easy to sew and washable. Scrunch a fabric in your hand to see if it creases easily.

Colour

Check that the colour suits you. Stand in front of a mirror and hold the fabric up to your face.

If the colour has to match other clothes, take them to the shop with you.

Artificial light can change the colour of a fabric. Ask the shop assistant if you can take it to a doorway or window to look at it in daylight.

Taking your measurements

To make your own clothes, you need to know your measurements. Patterns come in numbered, standard sizes, which are based on standard chest, waist and hip measurements.

All patterns allow some 'ease', so that the garments you make allow room for movement. You do not need to buy a size larger than you really take.

Before you start

Measure yourself in your underwear to get your accurate measurements.

You might find it helpful to ask a friend to take some of the measurements.

How to measure your chest, waist and hips

Measure your chest around the fullest part.

You can find your natural waistline by holding the tape measure loosely around your waist area and wriggling about a bit.

Measure your hips around the widest part when you are standing with your legs together.

Jot your measurements down and take them to the shop with you when you buy the pattern.

Other useful measurements

Your back length measurement is the distance between the bone at the base of your neck and your waist.

To find your sleeve length, bend your arm and measure from the top of your shoulder, over the curve of your elbow to your wrist.

You need to know your inside leg measurement when making trousers. Measure from your crotch to your ankle.

Finding your size

Look up your chest measurement on the chart. The waist and hip measurements should be about the same as yours too. Find out your size at the top of the chart.

	Metric Sizes				Imperial Sizes			
	8	10	12	14	8	10	12	14
Chest	80cm	83cm	87cm	92cm	31½"	32½"	34"	36"
Waist	61cm	64cm	67cm	71cm	24"	25"	26½"	28"
Hips	85cm	88cm	92cm	97cm	33½"	34½"	36"	38"

Understanding patterns

A pattern gives you a lot of information. Here are the main things you need to know.

The front of the pattern

If you have not made any clothes before, choose a simple pattern to start with and make sure you buy it for your size.

The back of the pattern

This gives you a brief description of the design.

View

A pattern sometimes gives you 2 or 3 versions of the same basic style. Check how much fabric you need for your version.

Suggested fabrics

It is best to choose one of the recommended fabrics.

Fabric width

Fabric is made in three standard widths: 90cm, 115cm and 150cm. The pattern tells you how much fabric you would need to buy in each width.

With/without nap

If your fabric has a nap, you will need more of it. The pattern tells you how much more.

The chart tells you how much fabric you need. Look up your size and the right version, the fabric width and with/without nap.

Notions

These are all the extra bits you need, such as zips and thread. Buy them with the fabric so that you can match the colours.

Restrictions

This tells you which fabrics to avoid using.

Inside the pattern

Inside the pattern you will find fabric layouts and step-by-step instructions.

Index

First published in 1985 by Usborne Publishing Ltd,
20 Garrick Street, London WC2E 9BJ, England
Copyright © 1985 Usborne Publishing Ltd

Printed in Belgium.